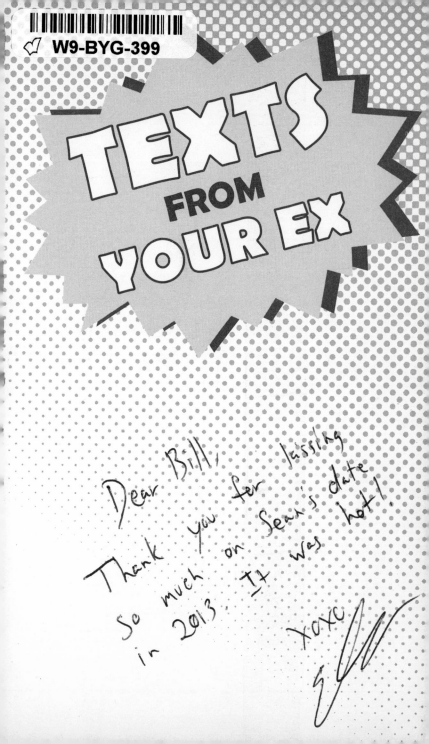

TEXTS
FROM
YOUR EX

Dear Bill,

Thank you for lassing
So much on Sean's date
in 2013. It was hot!

xoxo

TEXTS
FROM
YOUR EX

FROM THE
INSTAGRAM SENSATION BY
UNSPIRATIONAL

An Hachette UK Company
www.hachette.co.uk

First published in Great Britain in 2015 by
Hamlyn, a division of Octopus Publishing
Group Ltd
Carmelite House
50 Victoria Embankment
London, EC4Y 0DZ
www.octopusbooks.co.uk
www.octopusbooksusa.com

Distributed in the US by
Hachette Book Group
1290 Avenue of the Americas
4th and 5th Floors
New York, NY 10020

Distributed in Canada by
Canadian Manda Group
664 Annette St.
Toronto, Ontario, Canada M6S 2C8

ISBN 978-1-844-03878-7

A CIP catalogue record for this book is
available from the British Library

Printed and bound in UK

10 9 8 7 6 5 4 3 2 1

Commissioning Editor: Hannah Knowles
Editor: Pollyanna Poulter
Proofreader: Corinne Masciocchi
Art Director: Juliette Norsworthy
Designer: Geoff Fennell

Picture credits

Fotolia jorgenmac100 132;
williamrobson 58. **Getty
Images** jameslee1 8.
iStock DanBrandenburg
235. **Shutterstock** Evart
24; jmcdermottillo 3, 198;
johnkworks 70, 226;
studiostoks 6. **Thinkstock**
memoangeles 44; Valeriy
Kachaev 86.

CONTENTS

It's a beautiful night. The moon is full and there's a gentle breeze. You've had a great evening out with your friends. You had a delicious dinner and watched a funny movie and now you're home, settling into bed. Everything seems so perfect. What could possibly go wrong?

And then you hear it.

Your cell phone is vibrating on the table. But this vibration isn't like every other vibration.

There's something sinister about it. Something dark. Something evil.

A chill comes over your whole body and you feel like you're in a horror movie. A car alarm goes off. A coyote howls. What's happening? Why does everything suddenly feel so wrong?

You reach for your phone and there it is...

A TEXT...

...FROM YOUR EX

We all know the feeling. We all know what it's like to look down at our phone and see the one name we hoped we'd never see again, but here they are. Exes are a lot like cockroaches. They're disgusting, they're everywhere, and no matter what you do, you can never quite seem to kill them.

So instead of letting them torture us for all eternity, we decided to turn the tables. *Texts From Your Ex* was born as a reminder to every ex out there:

"You may be able to send me a message at 3am, but be careful, buddy, because you may just find your text being read by several million people the next day."

Texts From Your Ex is our one defense against all the jerkass exes of the world. Together, we battle the angry, the bitter, the sad, the jealous, the silly, the cheating, the vulgar, the shitty, shitty exes of this world and together, we laugh at them.

No longer will we be held hostage by the late-night drunken ramblings of somebody that we used to know.

So look out, exes, because the texts you send could soon become...

TEXTS FROM YOUR EX

AMNESIA

I wish you could forget my phone number the way you forget everything else.

Best ad for HBO ever

All questions. No answers

No one has EVER spelled reminiscing more incorrectly. EVER

Oh, that thing?

Hey I just wanted to say congratulations on the opening. I think about you a lot and hope you're doing well.

Seriously

I was just trying to be nice Helen, I'm sorry

So are you not going to respond

remember that one time you had me watch your dog, pick you up from the airport, rent a cabin and then tell me you hangout with your ex and are getting back with her? Ya, go fuck yourself

He's just being NICE, Helen. Gosh!

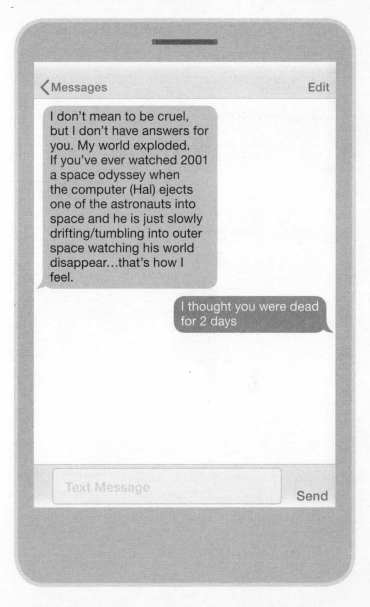

No one knows what's happening here

<Messages   Edit

I won't beg

I just don't want to lose u

> Maybe you'll actually spend that time you need alone now

I will and I have been

> Except when your tongue was stuck down that girl's throat and your hand was lodged in her anal cavity

Text Message   Send

Anal. Cavity.

A screenshot in a screenshot in a screenshot in a book. Meta

Messages Edit

You are in denial. We had good times together. I'd say all the time we had together was amazing and fun

Not denial just reality.

If right now, I said I would sell my house, quit my job, leave Sopehi, just to be with you, what would you say

Sophie

I'd say that you're a piece of shit. I'm pretty sure you guys have twins on the way

Text Message Send

World's Greatest Dad

Maybe next time put "I miss you" first

Oh yeah, I forgot about that

<Messages **Restraining Order** Edit

Happy new year

One time I made a giant mural and wrote that I loved you in giant letter in front of the highschool on the sidewalk and then it rained that night..

One time I told you to never text me again and you obviously still do............................

Text Message Send

This one time at band camp...

Thanks for letting me know. Always so good to hear from you

I always forget that I'm married!

BOOTY CALL

U Up?

That's no way to speak to a lord!

Fart. Box.

You don't take no for an answer, do you?
We've got to move on

**How fresh is this bikini wax really?
Whatever. This is nonsense**

That escalated quickly...

I'll be over in 5

**Does the fire indicate the burning
when you pee?**

if we'd hooked up you'd still be recovering ;)

Haha no I think it would be the other way around missy. I have a big 8" hammer. You have tiny hips..I have no idea how I'd even fit. And I'm not just saying it. I'd feel it would be too big for your little body

Hahahaha take care babe

Text Message

Send

We all feel terrible for you

They call me the space heater

This is a REALLY fun thing to do

Refollow. Refollow. REFOLLOW. ASAP

What kind of truck?

Crime and Punishment

Great visual

Sorry, Jason

Oh, in that case...

you just said you were gonna find someone else ...doesn't make me believe you care

Holy fuck all I want to know now is r we going to bang again

not if you have a girlfriend

Okay then nice talking to ya

fuck you

Text Message

Send

Wait, so you are going to fuck me?
IT'S ALL SO CONFUSING

Maybe if you just keep saying "love u"

DRUNK EXES

We've all been there. It's 3am and you just got home from the bar. You look at your phone. And then suddenly it's the next morning. **WHAT HAVE YOU DONE?**

Explain yourself now and immediately in complete detail and honesty, or I will trust my own heart, and leave without looking back.

There will be no friendship.

I am psychic and claisentient

This is how I know.

When ure fucking somebody

I feel everything

Text Message   Send

I AM CLAISENTIENT!!!

I am (not) drunk

You forgot?

Explanatoon!!!

Sometimes you just need ten shots of tequila before talking to someone

**Don't talk to me at 5am unless
you're handing me coffee**

Who dies in hell?

Nobody wany you

Let me spell it out for you

Are you sure? Drunk would be a good excuse

I don't think you need any more beer

Finally! Something to celebrate!

GIVE ME MY SHIT BACK

Some of the best things in life are free. And some of those things are just things exes left at your house. The spoils of war. These texts are from people who simply don't want to pay the break-up tax.

But seriously, did you take my flannel?

Is this about the flannel again?

Messages   **Ex Fiancé**   Edit

I'm in the area. Let me know if you're available.

Wrong person

Where's my blue bucket with all my bike rags and wash shit?

I want my Blu Ray movies back. You took every single one. And my micro fiber towels. And your half of the $300 for cleaning. And whatever the fuck else you weren't supposed to take.

Text Message   Send

"Micro Fiber?"

The dangers of dating a shepherd

**In this case, the "I hate you"
was BEFORE the breakup**

Ain't nobody got time for that

I don't give a shit but WHERE ARE THE FUCKING CANDLES?

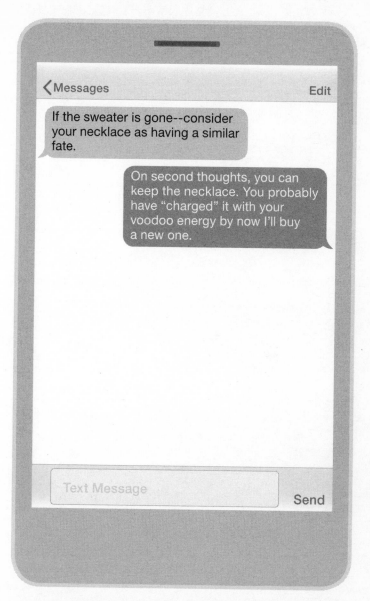

If the sweater is gone--consider your necklace as having a similar fate.

On second thoughts, you can keep the necklace. You probably have "charged" it with your voodoo energy by now I'll buy a new one.

Just out of curiosity, what is this guy doing with all the necklaces he collects?

**Always delete your sex tapes
BEFORE the break-up**

Sometimes you love them.
Sometimes you hate them.

Either way, you still have their
number and you're going to
make sure they know EXACTLY
how you feel about them!

70k? Holy shit!

If all your friends told you to find a cliff, would you?

Fuck your family!

I think they're talking about shit

What the fucj?

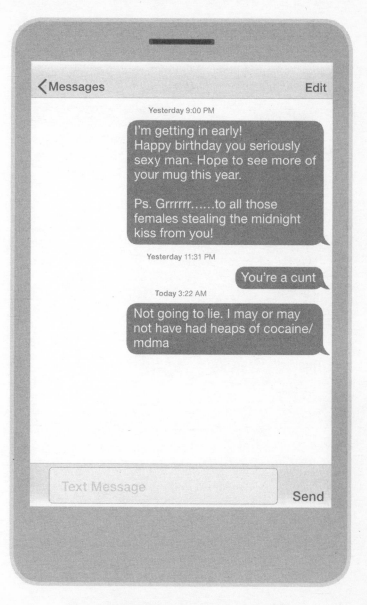

**You really shouldn't be taking
drugs in "heaps"**

Hi, Don!

Thank you for this conversation. It brought me closure. And for your information—I was with you because I felt safe in your innocence. I felt that connection and empathy that only comes along rarely in life. I'll ignore your "finger pointing"—eventually I think you'll realize has no weight. Be well. I will delete your contact information and prior communications. My last words: I love you.

Just so we're clear: I don't.

Text Message   Send

Why are you still talking?

You can't be one without the other

Romance is not dead. Yet

What kind of name is "Lol"?

Ah yes. The old broken-hearted hammer, syringe, shower, cigarette, train

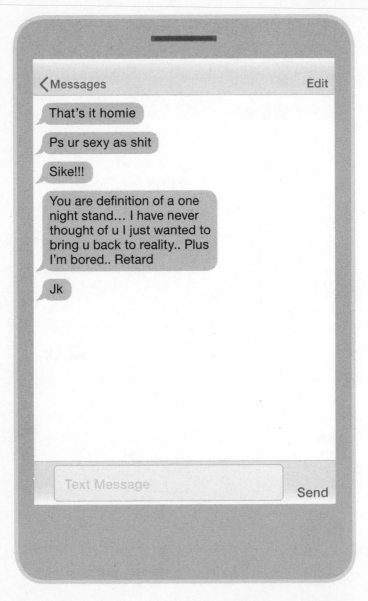

Hard to resist a man who calls you "homie"

PERSISTENCE

If at first you don't succeed, make a total ass out of yourself for several years.

Commitment

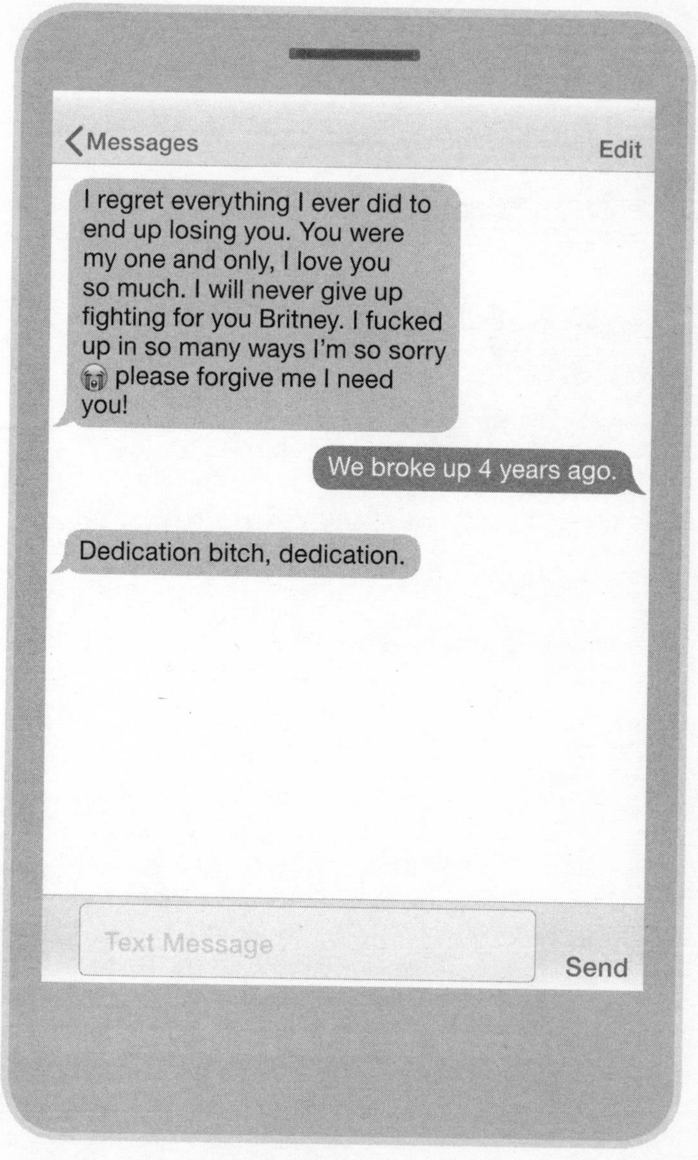

"Dedication, bitch"

You have anger issues so FUCK YOU

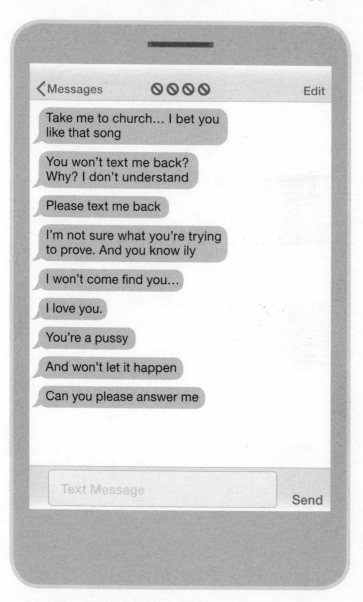

Not sure why she's not responding

Rock bottom: A fun place to live

This kind of bullshit is probably why she broke up with you

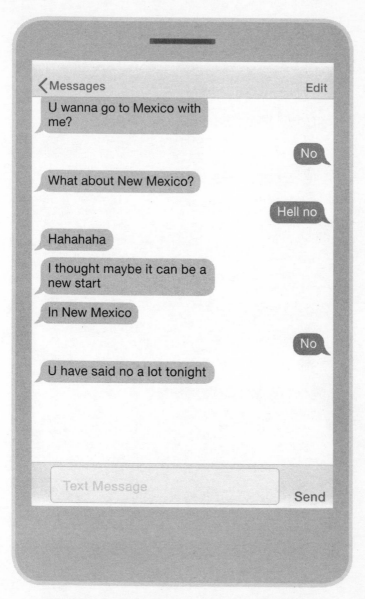

Ok, how about Super New Mexico?

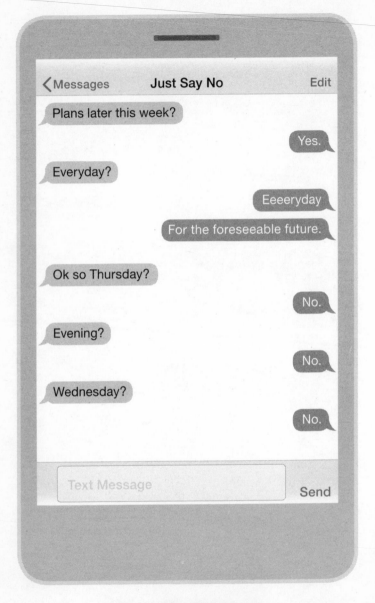

How about Friday?

Oh My God

From now on, I only respond in acronyms

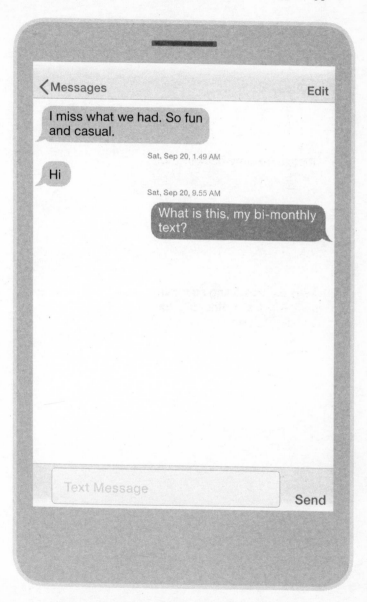

**Every other time I get my period,
this guy comes around**

Because DONE

**I'm trying to stalk you.
Why are you being difficult?**

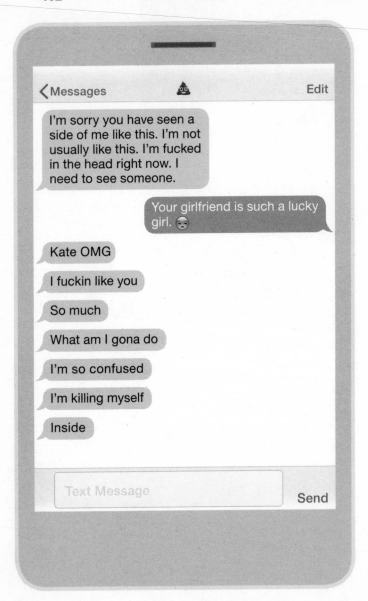

"Inside"

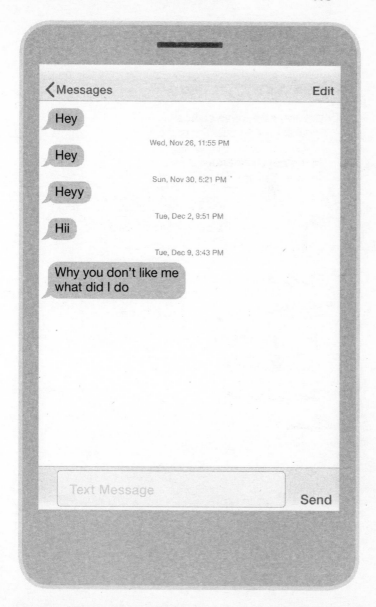

**Well, you're such a stunning conversationalist,
I can't imagine why she's not writing back**

You want what you can't have

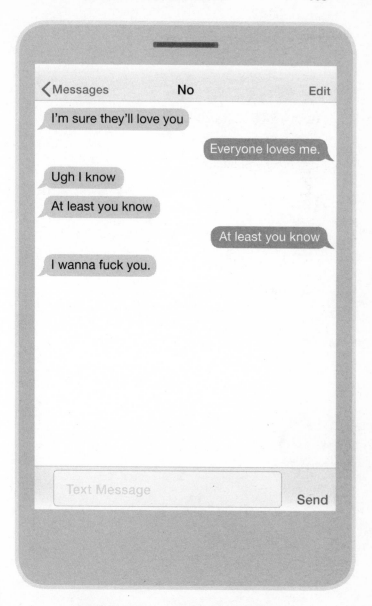

Well, that's unlikely to happen

**There's no way she actually
stopped texting**

Actually it was 1:36

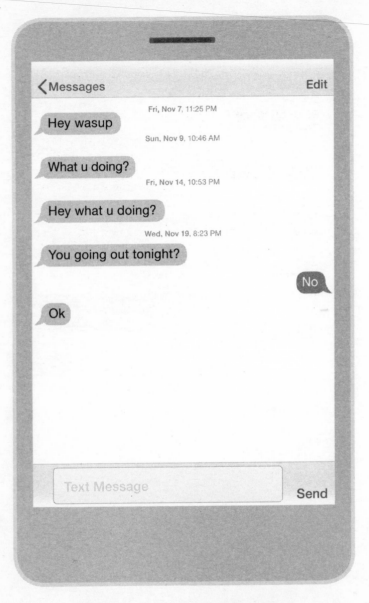

That was surprisingly easy

**He's been in that car outside
for 7 years now**

**For a guy who keeps such good track of dates,
I'm surprised he can't find his address book**

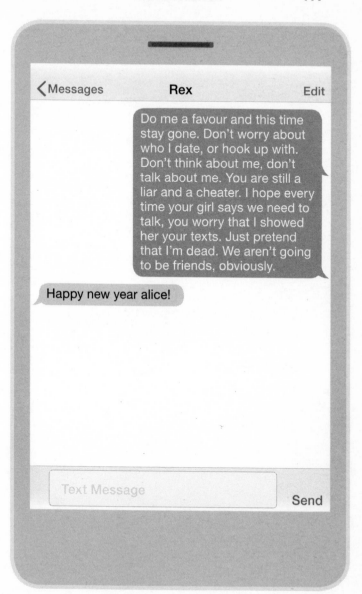

Do me a favour and this time stay gone. Don't worry about who I date, or hook up with. Don't think about me, don't talk about me. You are still a liar and a cheater. I hope every time your girl says we need to talk, you worry that I showed her your texts. Just pretend that I'm dead. We aren't going to be friends, obviously.

Happy new year alice!

Rex can't read

Much better than "I love you"

Sexts from your Ex

OK

1048

Come out. I'm with Koreans.

Seriously. It's pretty fun. See you here?

I know you're seeing this…

I'm moving to England in a month and I'd like for you to come with me.

Text Message Send

Wait, you're with Koreans? What does that mean?

"I'm busy that day"

And that's why you're crazy

Please stop

You are seriously deranged

I cut ties with you

While you blow me up

This is so dumb

Leave me alone

Don't talk to me

Don't come to my work

Idk why you even would want to

You never did before

Wait? You're asking ME to stop?

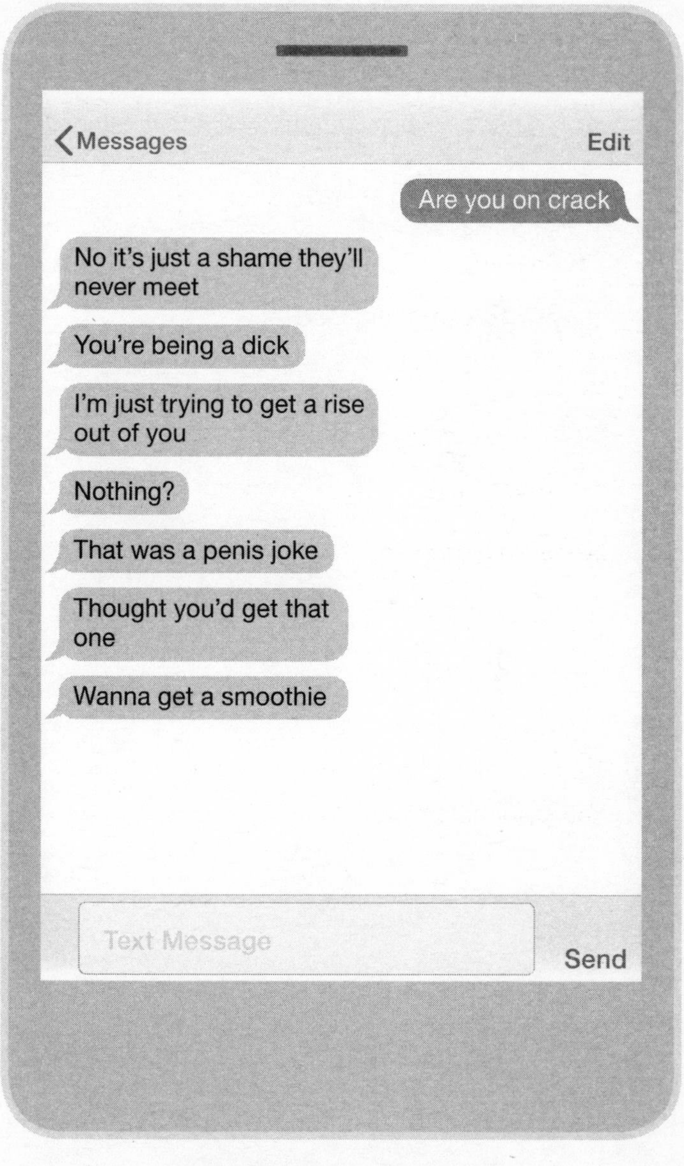

Are you on crack

No it's just a shame they'll never meet

You're being a dick

I'm just trying to get a rise out of you

Nothing?

That was a penis joke

Thought you'd get that one

Wanna get a smoothie

Text Message

Send

Yep. Definitely crack

She's like Hallmark

Brick wall waterfall, girl you think you know it all you don't I do, so pshhhhhh with that attitude. Peace, punch, captain crunch, I got something you can't touch, Reese's pieces, 7 up, Mess with me and I'll mess you up.

Oh okay. Good luck with all that.

Haha u suck

Jess just had a stroke

Stupidfuck

‹Messages   Edit

The fuck

If you had to say one positive thing about me, what would it be?

Like what do you think my best quality is as a person?

I think that yours is that you are super kind and generous

I also think that you have a good ass, but that's not really a quality as much as it is a physical attribute

Btw I still haven't heard about the fucking job. They made a decision Thursday

Text Message   Send

I would say your best quality would be that you're "relentless"

**A big fat juicy throbbing Christmas
to you as well**

Waiting up for the Wet Fart Fairy

I would never intentionally hurt you, I'd do anything to make you happy and that's the truth. Hope you realise that x

Please fuck off

Have you seen the Lord of the rings? Lol random question x

Text Message   Send

Shut the fuck up x

Microwave

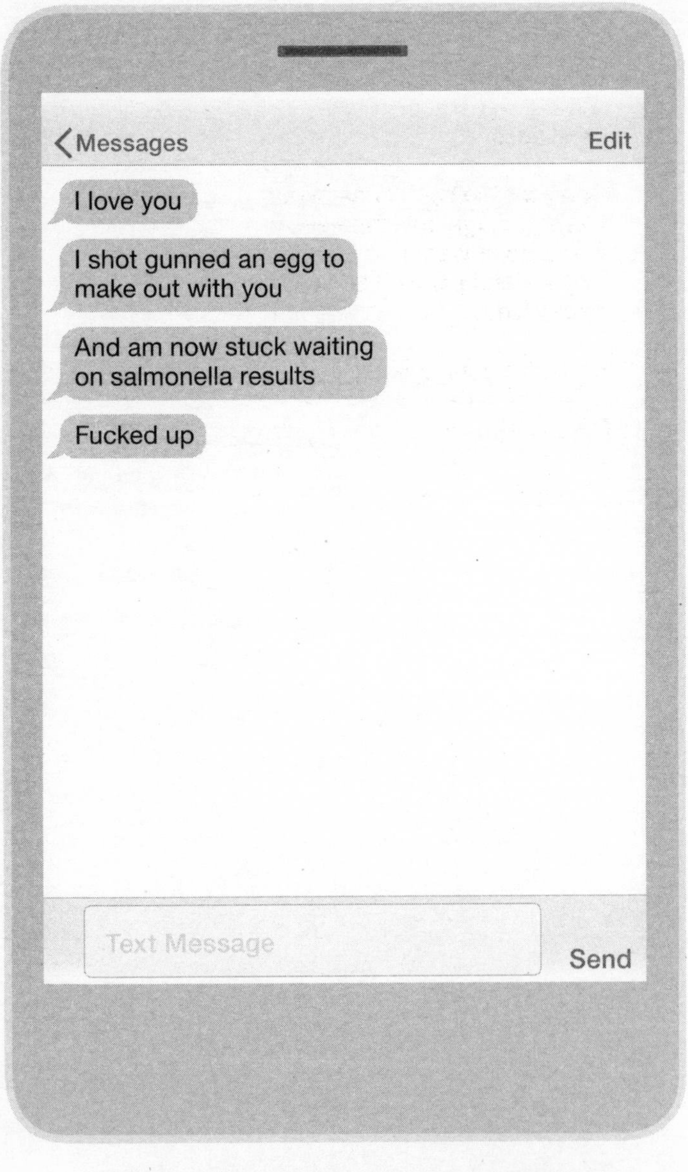

I love you

I shot gunned an egg to make out with you

And am now stuck waiting on salmonella results

Fucked up

Text Message

Send

WHAT THE FUCK IS HAPPENING IN THIS RELATIONSHIP?

Messages Edit

Sorry for the harshness of our last exchange. Feel bad about it and don't want it to be the way we end things. I sincerely apologize

I will take your lack of response as a "go to hell"

Text Message

Send

Good call

I was fine until you started texting me

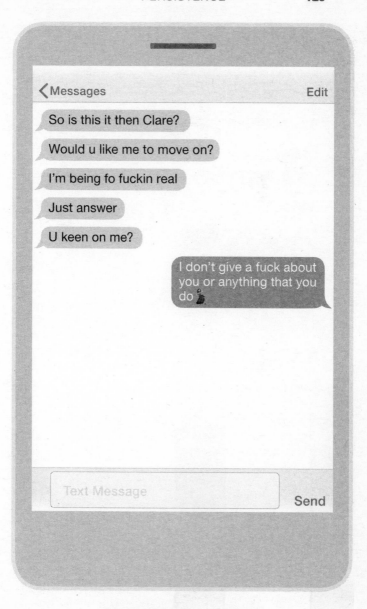

The emoji says it all

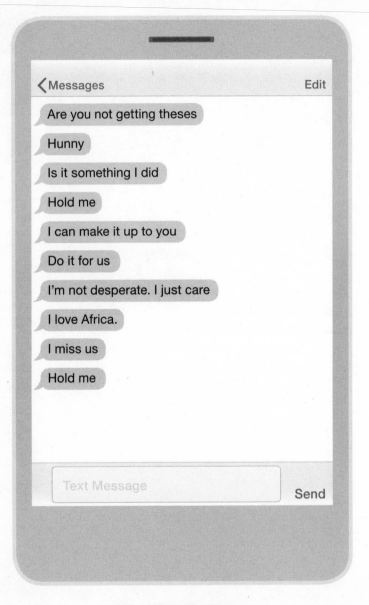

We all love Africa

SHUT DOWNS

Sometimes all you want to do is talk and sometimes all the other person wants you to do is shut the fuck up.

Turns out the best texts from exes are classic shut downs, so this is a bumper-edition chapter.

Everyone here is having fun

Messages   Edit

Hi Laura. I am driving with ray but have been meaning to send you a message for a while now and keep forgetting. But I just wanted to say that I will message you soon and I'm so sorry that we didn't talk after that night. You don't deserve that and you are an all round incredible person and the last thing I want to do is hurt you so I am so sorry if I did

Should I mail you your hat?

Text Message   Send

What kind of hat is it?

Granite

Fish hand!

For two people fighting, there's a lot of agreeing going on

**Nothing says "I can protect you"
like the crying emoji face**

I do. Learn to give peace a chance. It's uplifting. You'd like it.

Doubt is not peace.

Stop fucking texting me you self absorbed asshole.

Just go die

Bye

Text Message   Send

Bono, is that you?

Lee is a little girl with little girl dreams

That's one small step for man and one giant leap out of this conversation

Russia is beautiful this time of year

Fluff and Fold and Fire

Yeah, "Adam"

Hopefully I'll be lucky enough to never hear from you again

<Messages   Edit

> Ok. I won't contact you. But when you finally do meet a nice guy, make sure you give him a fair chance. Don't judge him based off of my actions of being an asshole. It's not fair to him.

> Wow how sweet of you thanks. Fuck off.

Text Message   Send

Thanks, Tony Robbins

You're the summer breeze in my ear drums

I'm the knife to your throat if you don't stop texting me

Text Message   Send

Poetry

Go fuck yourself, Seanybear is just fun to say

Probably

Messages **Random Ass Mother Fu...** Edit

We should link up on campus?

Seriously fuck off and delete my number

Text Message

Send

**That's a very exotic name.
Where are your parents from?**

That's what breaking up is. Now, go away

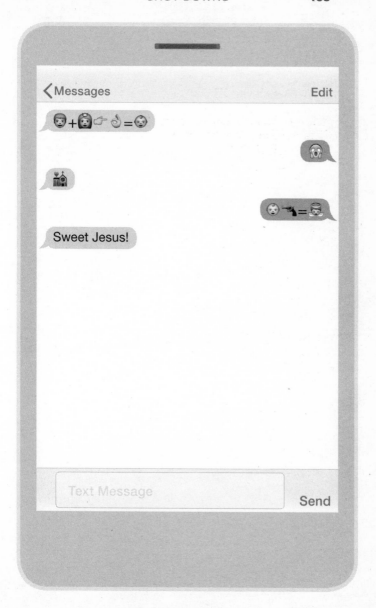

Angel kill baby?

Let's not and say we did

Honesty is important

Maybe tomorrow, Satan

Dicklick

all I want in life is to make out with you, bang you, and occasionally cuddle you.

Do you know any kush dealers?

I feel like we just want different things in life

I mean I have thought about what I could do to put a smile on your face and me be the first thing you think about when you wake in the morning with a smile on your face

I already have something special in my life that does that for me...

It's called coffee

Text Message   Send

I totally thought she was going to say "a vibrator"

**Manual read receipts are
super fuck you**

Doing "well," Satan

It's the most wonderful time of the year

Home is where the heart is

Not with those nugget fingers

RIP best friend's sister's cousin's uncle's wife's daughter's boyfriend's dog

**These both just seem like terrible people.
They should get back together**

I made tuna salad! You can do both!

You'll be up all night waiting for Santa

Oh...ok... I'm sorry. So, do you want me to stop texting you?

That is interesting. It is

YES

Same desire. Different reasons

Walked right into that one

you're skinny and pretty so you're used to getting away with things but I want you to know that your actions have effects on others, and I hate you. You are a horrible person and you not understanding that you're a horrible person doesn't make you less of a horrible person

I stopped at skinny and pretty

Text Message

Send

Only read the words you like

But are you on LinkedIn?

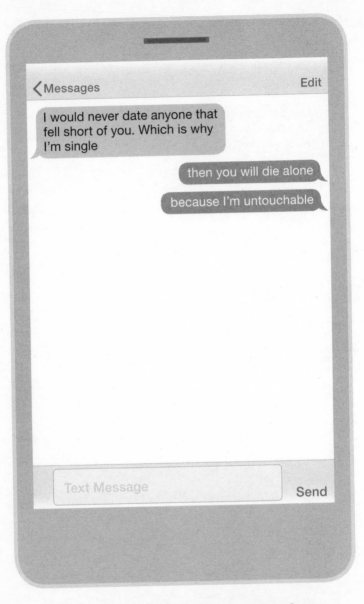

I would never date anyone that fell short of you. Which is why I'm single

then you will die alone

because I'm untouchable

Dying alone actually sounds okay after talking to you

Baby. Carrots.

YES A LOT OF THINGS WOULD BE NICE

Solid advice

#YONO

Never trust a Fuckboy

Ice, Ice, Baby

Stop, you're making me blush

I'm sorry i cheated on you!! But just because i screwed up once you all of a sudden think you're better than me?!

is that what this is huh?! you think you're better than me?!

i know I am. bye.

Text Message

Send

I don't think she's over it

I'm not loving anyone else, dating anyone or spoiling anyone

You have someone that treats you better

So obviously you moved on a long time ago

🎈🎈🎈🎈🎈 here are some balloons for your pity party

Text Message

Send

Have a great party, Cunt

At least we agree on something

Is that a yes?

Way to fight for love, Jay

Ex Tip: Check in every six months

I'm sorry for everything. You were a good guy that I took advantage of. I was dumb for letting you go. I wake up every morning thinking of how much I miss you. Please give "us" another chance?

Who's this?

Really Jason?

I hope you feel stupid right now, like you made me look. Rot in hell you dick juggling thundercunt!

Dick Juggling Thundercunt was my nickname in high school

So......... maybe?

I know u prob have me blocked but just want to wish you a happy belated birthday and tell you that I'm always here for you.

Oops guess I didn't block you on my new phone thanks for the reminder to do so

Text Message

Send

New phone. Old exes

Messages   Edit

The only thing is that I have a lot of fun. I'm so excited to be the best of the best. I love you so much better than the original version of this year. I'm at work today and I'm still waiting for the next few weeks of school for a while and then you will never understand how much I love the way you want to go home and watch movies. Really fun to watch this movie and the rest of my favourite song. !!

Sorry new phone who is this

Text Message

Send

Are you having a seizure?

The anticipation is killing me

THAT. HURTS. A. LOT.

Talk to the hand

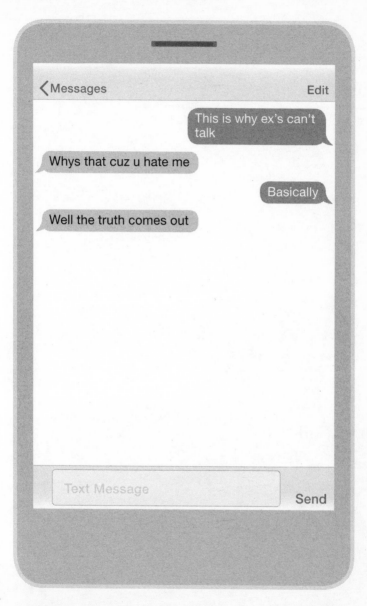

We are all so thankful that exes CAN talk

**You've moved on with your life,
but they haven't.
And maybe they never will.**

Get back to me when it's over

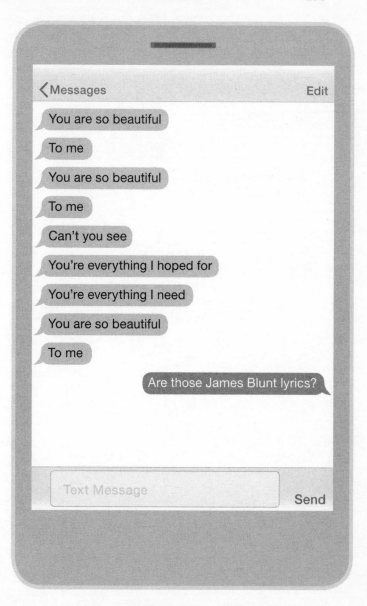

Actually, it's Joe Cocker

I'm more of a hip-hop fan

<Messages **Stupidbitch DONTDOIT** Edit

This has been getting harder every day since you texted me on Monday

I hate pretending I'm okay. I miss you

I'll pray for you.

Text Message

Send

Oh good, that should help

**You're the only person on Earth
who's ever seen Flubber**

**Wish in one hand. Shit in the other.
See which one fills up first**

Sat, Oct 18, 3:05 AM

Please give me another chance.
Life is meaningless without you.

Sat, Oct 18, 8:41 AM

Disregard.

Messages   **Dirtbag**   Edit

Text Message   Send

No problem

How do you even pronounce that name?

And now you can say "bye"

Take a Xanax, Fuckboy

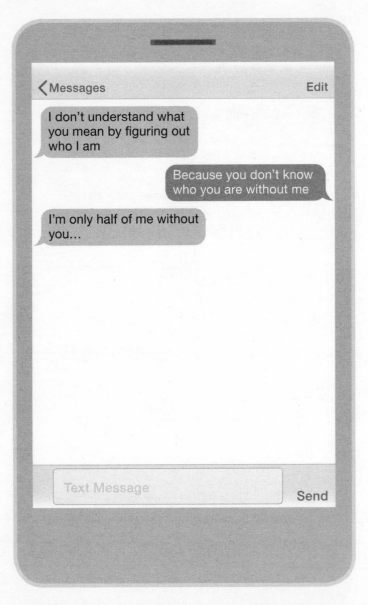

Stop watching Bridges of Madison County

Agree to agree

Is it bad that I miss dating you?

Is it bad the only thing I miss about dating you was getting my food paid for?

Text Message   Send

The Hunger Games

Choose your own adventure

Then what?

OBVIOUSLY

It was a really nice wallet

You'll find out what it is very soon

Try again tomorrow

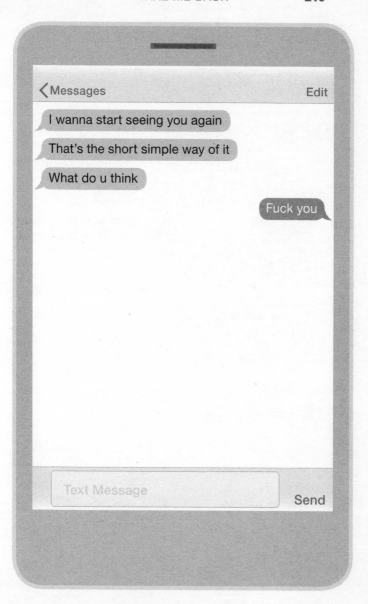

Short and simple

GET A LIFE, RICK

The lamest thesaurus of all time

Troy ofunkynutz

< Messages   Edit

Having fun with hockey buddys

What's the big deal

Broke my heart

Sun, Sep 28, 8:55 PM

Think about you all day

Mon, Sep 29, 6:15 PM

Come to Calgary

Wed, Oct 1, 11:44 PM

You have mono?

?

Text Message   Send

One too many hits to the head there, Troy

Very serial killery of you

You forgot your ex-girlfriend's name, didn't you?

Touché

She's flattered

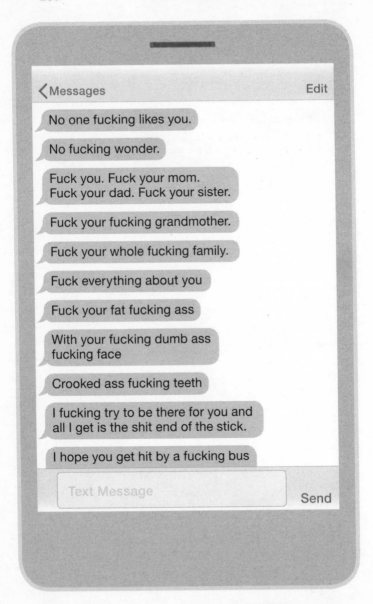

At least he's committed to something

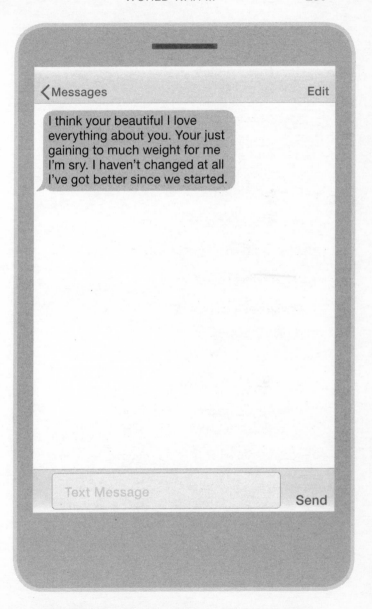

You've gotten better? We still think there's room for improvement

<Messages      Edit

> People keep asking what happened between us

Tell them the truth

> Okay...

WHY ARE YOU TELLING PEOPLE IM A LITTLE BITCH AND THAT'S WHY WE BROKE UP!!?!

> You said tell the truth...

Text Message   Send

The truth hurts

**Okay but if I killed you
will you stop texting me?**

You might think that's funny but that's actually a criminal offense. Thanks for the evidence!!!!

Hahaha wow no it isn't it's my bear u can't prove it

Your crazy

Text Message

Send

What did the bear ever do to you?

Ten teenage girls wrote this reply and died from laughing too hard

**We found someone who's actually
a bigger prick than their attorney**

Your stupid

Oh hey btw your dick has ruined my life

I've been missing my soul for awhile now I think

Lol I would apologize for that but we both know I'm not really that sorry.

I literally fucking hate you

That's unnecessary

But thanks I hate you more 🖤

Text Message   Send

Literally

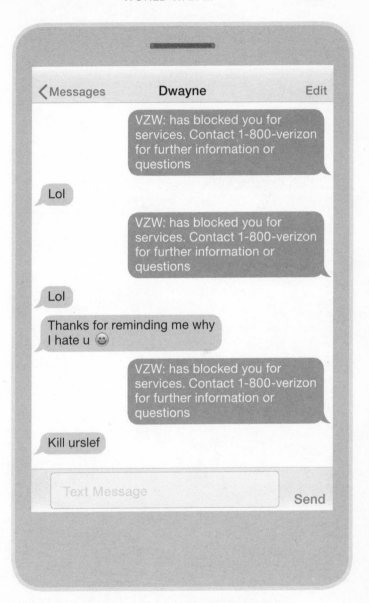

Go fuck urslef, Dwayne

No literally actually fuck off

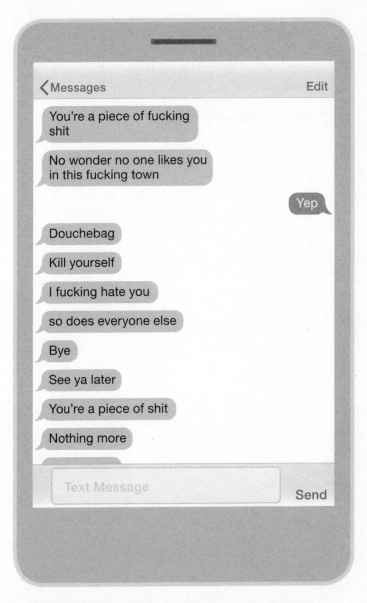

We like how there's obviously something more after "nothing more"

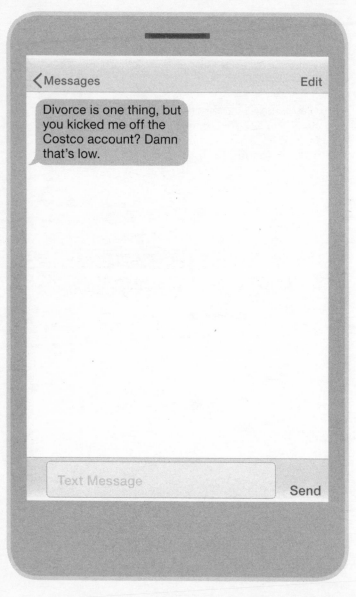

Buy your tissues in bulk

And you're also broke and part of the past

So you're doing well I take it?

Well, there's always next year

**The 11th commandment is
"Thou Shalt Not Block on Instagram"**

Messages ⟨   Edit

It's fine you can have her. Hope y'all are happy together in your white trash dirty talk mansion. Goodbye.

Who y'all calling white trash while throwing the term y'all around like that

I SAID GOODBYE

Fine. But stop YELLING AT ME

Text Message   Send

I SAID GOOD DAY, SIR!

**I'm starting to think these emoji
are passive-aggressive**

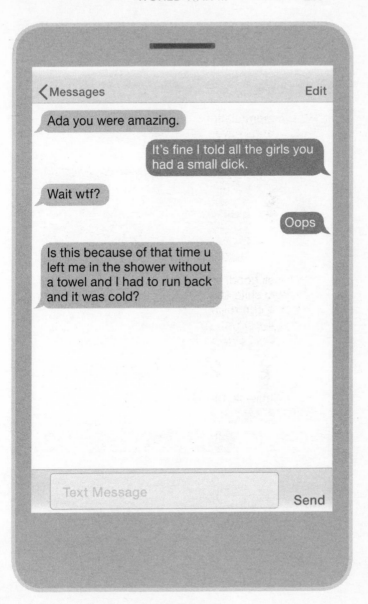

Shrinkage!

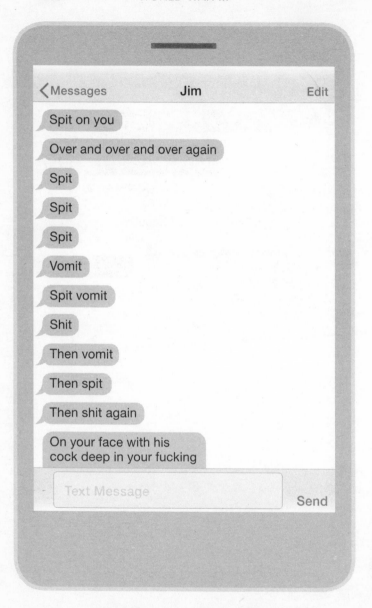

Maybe take a nap, Jim

Seems like maybe no one loves you

**He's moving to LA. He's going to be a star.
What could go wrong?**

Sometimes we all have to take the trash out

About the author

Established in 2014, Unspirational is a dark and mysterious force hell-bent on the eradication of misguided positivity and aiming to provide the world with humour through morbidity, negativity, and brutal honesty. It was founded by social media phenom and television producer, Elan Gale, who still doesn't know what he wants to be when he grows up.

Acknowledgments

Unspirational would like to thank our fearless leader, Elan Gale, whose cynicism and morbidity are the source of all our darkness. We would also like to thank Bill Dixon, whose tireless efforts and humor keep us laughing every day. Finally, we would like to thank Matt Wise, Hannah Knowles, Foundry, and Octopus Books for having the creativity to see an Instagram Page and make it into a hit book that you just paid money for and are currently reading.

Lastly, to all the happy, optimistic, excited go-getters out there…

Get real. We're all going to die soon.